Hmmm!!!

LESSONS LEARNED

Susan Derington

Printed in the United States of America by

H.V. CHAPMAN & SONS
BOOKBINDERS | PRINTING | PROMOTIONAL PRODUCTS

802 North Third Street
Abilene, Texas 79601
www.hvc-ram.com

ISBN: 978-1-940850-80-1
First Paperback Edition

10 9 8 7 6 5 4 3 2 1

The paper used in this publication meets the minimum requirements of ANSI/ NISO Z39.48-1992 (R 1997) (Permanence of Paper). ∞

DEDICATED TO MY BOYS:

Chad and Jason Montgomery

THIS BOOK OF POEMS HAS EVOLVED OVER A PERIOD OF 50 YEARS OF MY LIFE.

THEY EXPRESS MY LESSONS LEARNED AND HOPEFULLY YOU WILL ENJOY THEM IN THEIR SIMPLICITY.

I LOVE YOU

Mom

MY NOTES:

There is no time like the present to begin your journey with Infinity.

Take what you have learned to others so they too may experience "joy, hope, peace" the wonderful presence of Life in every moment of every day.

Someone must speak the truth! Every person has been given the gift of Life within them. It waits for us to allow our old ideas to fade away as we believe in the power of Its truth.

The Divine Spirit will lead us daily. All criticism, judgmental attitudes, anger, resentment, jealousy will pass away. These will be replaced with encouragement, love, peace, loving others as ourselves completely -just because.

The ways of this world will die and only the power and love of our Divine Father will live forever.

LOVE

A touch, a life, a windblown hair

A feeling which comes from somewhere

God only knows it's there

To teach you and I to care.

Don't blink, you'll miss the power of it.

A smile, a gesture, a sound

Cherish it, nurture it, pray for more

Your abundance to be found

Share all around.

Without a single word,

True love will surely abound ...

A BETTER DAY

You sit very comfortably in your chair

Always wishing someone was there

The sound of a car

They cannot be far

In they walk, your heart beats so

As you gently say "hello"

How was your day?

(That's what you say)

Only to your dismay

Their eyes seem tired

No happiness at all

As they stand there in the hall

Come on in! Let's play!

There will be a Better Day.

ABANDONED

They drop me off and say

It will be better today

You'll go to school

Meet new friends

As they drive off on their way

The tears well up

My heart is broken

So many things left unspoken

I don't know what I did or said

Perhaps forgot to make my bed

Please give me another chance

Then you can teach me how to dance!

APOLOGY

Can you please accept my apology?

As I journey to find the "real" me

There are times I seem so out of control

It isn't a pretty sight to behold

Reactions bring forth memories of times gone by

My behavior seems to just fly, fly

The thoughts inside play tricks on me

Again, please accept MY apology!

ANGER

Once my enemy, now a friend
My strongest rival - scared.
A definite "NO -NO" right to the end
Always hidden, never shared

Now, I find for peace of mind,
Anger my friend must be
For without its waging
Against the raging
Lies that effect you and me
We're never free.

I'm amazed the lies to myself I've told
Kept me crippled, never bold

For to never be angry leaves things unsaid.
Builds walls that stifle one instead.

Makes one feel very cold.

AWAKEN

Awaken new - in peace, be still

You have learned to live His will

The calm quiet mind you have within

Will take away all bad thoughts

They cannot begin

Your only thoughts being of love and harmony

To be as God made you totally free

Just think of this possibility

Such a beautiful awakening ....

THE BEST IS YET TO COME!

The best is yet to come

With every new day

Come what may

The best is yet to come

Decisions, desires, excitement of life

Not a daily toiling, living in strife

The best is yet to come

The choices we make with the world at our feet

How marvelously complete!

The best is yet to come

BLAME

It's such a shame

To blame

Let us take responsibility for our own behavior

You can change problems you procure

Be strong and face yourself, don't waiver

Then you can endure

We are imperfect as you know

No matter how hard we try

So, on and on we go

Blaming others, why?

Days we live can be such a joy even with tribulation

As we do our very best

With greater expectation

This is not a time to jest

It is such a shame

To blame!

CAREFREE

What is it just to be carefree?
It is to just be

Work or play, enjoy it all
Let there be no time to stall

Life is too short, no time to waste
And yet don't live it in such haste

Flow with every waking day
Sharing your love along the way

Simply do your best
Knowing there'll be time to rest

Enjoy the fact that you can live
Learning ways in which to give

Your very best---- carefree!

CHANGE

THERE ARE TIMES TO STOP AND CONSIDER WHICH
DIRECTION YOUR LIFE IS GOING

NOT TO BECOME BITTER

THE TIME TO KEEP ON GROWING.

COULD YOU LEARN TO ENJOY THE WORST AS THOUGH IT
WERE A BURST

OF LIVING

JUST KEEP ON GIVING?

I'M NOT SUGGESTING FANTASY TO SUCH A DEGREE

INSTEAD ------------------REALITY!!!

A CHILD

I'm so innocent and yet
I never can forget

The loud voices you and Daddy had
It really made me very sad
I prefer it when you're happy, not mad

Still I go on, yet with increased fear
And really need you very near.

My life is just beginning, surely you can see
I'm trying hard to just be me
Please help me to stay free,
No more anxiety.

THE CHRISTMAS TREE

Were

I to be

A Christmas

tree, How perfect

I should like to be

with shining decorations

and lights aglow, and

feathers of birds quite lovely

to show. Beads of silver,

gold and red draped softly

as covers 'round my head.

HOW

WONDERFUL

TO BE

A

CHRISTMAS

TREE!!

COLD

It's cold outside, please come on in

We'll find a place here in the den

We can sit and visit about things new

Have hot chocolate and marshmallows, too

Let the fireplace take out the chill

Relax with a wrap, be really still

Ahhh, the wonderful warmth we feel.

CONTENT TO BE ME

I'm probably a 7 on a scale of 1 to 10
That's from the outside looking in
But should you find time to get to know me,
You'd soon discover just what I'd be

A complex mixture of you and you
And quite amazing, right out of the blue
You'll find it true.
We're all a mixture of me and you

So, should I decide to dislike you in your
own private ways,
Sooner or later in my days
I'm sure to see the "likes o' you" right
here within me.

It would be best for us both if I remain content
For you to be you and I to be me.
Knowing both are heaven sent
And though alike, as different as can be.

CURIOSITY

Curiosity is natural as we start our new life

Originally with very little strife

Then "should's" and "should-nots" raise their little heads

Fears, doubts and worries start shaking our beds

With no knowledge that we have control over them

These emotional feelings begin living within

Until one day the "truth" comes around

Freedom, courage and curiosity once again abound

DANCE

There is only one way to truly dance

Join the one you love as in a trance

Your movements together can be fast or slow

But always you will really know

Together, in love the only way to be

Sharing one another's destiny

With movements and rhythms of Joy's delight

Knowing no thing or no one can steal your light

It is given to all from Divine vibration

Now you can live in celebration!!!

DETERMINATION

Let us give an explanation

To this word "determination"

What it does <u>not</u> mean is "perhaps"

or "maybe" as some might wish to say

We are living and achieving it today

It is so easy to portray

Staying focused is our treasure

Only then can we achieve

That in which we believe.

Then we will find our measure

Determination to conceive

A DREAM

Reality or fantasy??
A lifetime of questions for you and me.

We take the road we "know" is right
Then find ourselves in quite a fright
Running, running in the night.

Surely the other turn would be much better
For comfort's sake, let's take a sweater.

Oh no ---it's hot, not cold at all
They promised Winter, yet it's still Fall.

The beginning road was life for me,
Yet in my journey to be free,
I chose right, then left, only to find
Quite deep within my mind

Fantasies, imaginings
The beginning road -the true thing!!

EGO

Our perception of reality

The strength to live each day

Works to build a life worthwhile

Hopes everyone will say

His life is so special

He's quite strong, you see

What a wonderful person, he's better than me

But God is still waiting for him to desire

A life led by Him so He can inspire

Happiness and peace throughout his days

As He leads him through life and is given the praise!

Ego set aside, God in control

One of the best stories ever told.

ENERGY

It's within, without, all around us to enjoy

Feel it, treasure it, begin to employ

The strength in your body as the chills race your spine

It is absolutely Divine!

Take its power with you everywhere

It gives you strength to share

There is enough for all

Each must answer His call

Know the energy is there

Nothing, nothing will compare

To His care.

FAITH

Unseen

Felt

Lived

Conquering

Conveying

Always saying ...

Go forth

Believe

Perceive

Listen

Hear

Respond

Share ALL in God's wonderful bond.

FEAR AND ANXIETY

Facing our emotions of fear and anxiety

Begin a process to becoming free

Those thoughts which cripple us each day

Can take our total joy away

First, we must see our self in truth

Face each fear and let it pass

Walk with faith right on through

Always knowing our strength will last

Anxiety and fears now are gone

We can be on our way home.

Peaceful thoughts take their place

We can smile, a happy face!

Be thankful!

A FRIEND

To have a friend, we must be one
A sensitive listening ear
A quiet word of cheer

That is a friend

A soul longing to be heard,
And yet without a word
A friend calls.

My spirit, how it soars
When through my doors
Comes the precious smile and love of my friend.

A gentle touch, a nudge,
He never would begrudge
My being me.

A calm and quiet sigh
As a friend passes by.

What a warmth I can feel!

I know it is real.

That wonderful, caring touch of my friend.

GAME

Life is a game

It's such a shame

We forget what's at hand

It's like some quicksand

The moments are gone

And before too long

We wonder where they went

The time is spent

We could have shared

Nothing would have compared

To the game of love had we dared.

I AM

I AM, He said!

As we rise from our bed

Take a moment or two

To talk to YOU.

Because you see inside your heart

Is where I've been right from the start

Say hello to Me before you begin this day

Then as you go, I will show you the way

Hand in hand we will walk

Arm in arm as we talk

I AM -- THROUGH YOU-- "I AM"

IMAGINATION

Mmmmm - what can there be
So much to see
In my imagination

Health, wealth, an abundance of all
Yet we might be afraid we'll fall

I see hundreds of people smiling in delight
My, it's quite a sight!
In my imagination

No anger, frustration, worry, or dread
My God .... this must be heaven instead

Laughter, joy, love everywhere
Not a trial nor a care
In my imagination.

IS IT???

Is it true what others believe of you!

Is it!

Is it even true what you believe about you?

Is it?

We are such winners in our own way

Expressing ourselves with each passing day

What difference does it make what others may say?

Live your life to the fullest degree

Moment by moment as you are meant to be

Definitely becoming your real "ME".

I'M HERE

In case you didn't see me, "I'm Here"
Really quite near!

We get so stuck in ourselves, trying to be
perfect and content
When the message should be strongly sent

"I see you, I'm here"

We're all a part of God's heart
And need to show our best part

By noticing our brothers and sisters who say,

"Hey, I'm Here, Today!!!"

IN MY LATTER YEARS

My Father in heaven wanted me to see
It is never too late to be set free

My thoughts, my mind completely at rest
He has given to me His very best

Peace and love, what more could I share
His perfect gifts will always be here

They're within my reach as I look inside
He will always there abide

Within these years I've lost my fears
Through many, many floods of tears

To find self-control, in God's great Son
He is truly the only One.

In my latter years.

IT'S SO VERY HARD TO SEE

It's difficult to see through all the cracks in me

Like a window pane pure and clear

'til the stone was thrown so near

Vision soon would disappear.

Now replacement can be made

As we wait peacefully in the shade

Watching healing from the One

The Divine, God's Son!!

IT IS THE SPIRIT

It isn't the words coming from your mouth

That reach their destination

It's the Spirit in which they are spoken

Feelings that are broken

Coming from within to without

This changes the situation

Words are void and plain

Spoken in vain

Unless the caring Spirit nurtures you

And the words have become true

Being the REAL YOU!

JUST ANOTHER DAY

It's just another day, you say with dismay

OR

Hey! It's another day- Hooray!

Healthy, wealthy or not

You're in just the right spot

To begin this day another way.

This is the time to rejoice

You know, it's really your choice

To be sad, dreary

Weak and weary

OR

Smile with you heart

Right from the start.

Thankful you have been given

A reason for living

This wonderful "Just Another Day".

JUST "BE"

Have faith in yourself "Just be"

It will come so naturally

The Divine Father in you cannot be stopped.

Just ask and believe is what He says to do

He can certainly see you through.

Your talents cannot be blocked.

<u>Just be</u>.

LIFE

Whatever you do
See it through

A football game
A call to fame

It doesn't matter what you do,
But always see it through.

Don't give up midway
Finding a place to stay
And simply hide away.

Pursue your best!
That's the test

Beginning a better way.

LISTEN

The best of life is within our reach

If we'll but silent be

Slip outside very quietly

Listen to the tree

Reach high and pick a peach

Touch it, taste it, enjoy its flavor

Appreciate its beauty

Don't think it a duty

To pick the fruit of nature's best

Though there is little time for rest

These are the times to savor.

THE MIND

The mind I gave you is perfectly made

Throughout your life you can become dismayed

It is filled with lies, some truths, some twists

As Wisdom comes, you know those exist

Now, time for you to take control

Rid yourself of lies; only truths to behold

Living in peace, joy, and happiness

Without any doubt, you will become a success!!

Clearly seeing how you have been blessed.

ONE IN A MILLION

That friend so dear - one in a million

Stands ready to cheer

Encourage you as you walk on your way

Comforting, praying for you to have a better day

Sometimes with very little to say

The strength is there without a sound

Such a TRUE FRIEND you've surely found.

That special "one in a million"!!

ONION

The layers are peeled off one at a time to get where we are
going

God shows us how to do it, no bruising ever showing

How lovely as this change takes place

Revealing a precious center

Anointed with His amazing grace

Still there could be a splinter

He'll remove that, too as time goes by

Leaving only the best we are

He will give us another try

Healing the tiny scar ...

OUR CROSS

The cross we bear is within ourselves

We all have these "little elves"

Coming with thoughts both good and bad

Seizing our response whether happy or sad

It's our choice to take a look

As we work, write, or read a book

Change our thoughts to bring us pleasure

Enjoy our opportunities for leisure

Self-control of our thinking

Without blinking

Our Cross

OUR PLAY

We are in a play

Someone may say

As we perceive each wonderful day

We write the script as we go

With our "ups" and "downs", we will glow

Our rights, our wrongs, still our light will show

It cannot be hidden away for long

For we will soon again sing our song

Love tells us where we belong

As we live our very special play.

Come what may.

PEACE-BE STILL

Peace be still, goes against our will

As we hurry, hurry, hurry, never standing still.

It's no wonder we lose direction

In our searching for perfection

To hear the voice of Divinity

We must absolutely STOP-be still.

Listen to that "still small voice" and feel, feel the thrill

Of our Father's will.

PICTURE ME!

Can you picture me there in that tree?

I'm so thankful that I can see

The clouds as beautiful as can be!

Floating with the wind, making art in the sky

As they slowly are passing by

How I wish that I could fly

The grass around is tall and green

There is nothing in between

It is such an amazing scene

The cattle are eating and the deer as well

God's special plan will prevail

The indescribable beauty is hard to tell.

PRIDE

No one wants to speak his name

He is only wanting his Hall of Fame

No care for others, simply him you see

Nothing else matters just his destiny

He is harsh and self-centered, cannot seem to find

The love that exists deep in our mind

It can wash him away

He can no longer stay

He will leave as we pray.

PURIFICATION

Take an eye from me

So, I cannot see

Take an ear from me

So, I cannot hear

Take my tongue from me so I cause no fear

Simply help me to draw You near

God's Wonderful Love

QUESTIONS?

Where are we going?

What are we doing?

How will we get there?

What should we say?

PLEASE - GIVE US THE ANSWERS AS WE GO

ON OUR WAY

Relax and enjoy the trip, you see

All the answers will come to you "Free"

No need for such anxiety.

RAINDROPS

If You should but a raindrop be

Tossed upon a stormy sea

Flowing up and down, all around

Nowhere to be found

The wind stands still

The waves subside

There you will see "I" do abide

Peace be still, your God would say

In HIS very special way

You find yourself as YOU were made

Pure whole ... no longer afraid.

REST

Yes, take a day and make it your best

This is the wonderful time to rest

Quiet your mind and stop your feet

Now to feel you are complete

Enjoy this time while you prepare

To begin tomorrow and go somewhere

Rest gives new strength to get you there

Tomorrow will come and it will go

You'll do so much better as you well know

Simply because you took the time to REST.

A RING

When that special person comes along

Our hearts beat so loudly

Sing a sweet song

We think of the day we'll wear their ring

And hope it will be the real thing.

Growing in Love day after day

Supporting one another along the way

Aging together, as time passes by

The joy of it all makes one want to cry.

THE ROSE

Life is as the rose.

For some the bud dies before it is fully grown

For others it will open with very little foliage

For those chosen few, it will open fully in all its beauty

There are so many colors

Each one special in its own way,

But my favorite is the velvet red rose

Whose shadowing petals speak of its maturity.

SECRECY

We can hide these things inside of us

Refuse to let them heal

Be quiet and so secret about the way we truly feel

It's almost like a game we play

To keep hidden those thoughts we choose

Without true expression

We give the wrong impression

We will surely lose

SEEK

We'll find ourselves as life goes on
Though oft as not we feel alone

Comparisons are made with friends and foes
To fill our minds with fields of woes

Questions as "Are we more or less?"
Or "Are we truly our very best?"

I'd like it more to be expressed
As a field of flowers in the wilderness

Swaying gently with the current of air
Never feeling a need to beware or take care

Knowing nature's way of simplicity
Brings the rain to help us see
The strength inside both You and Me.

SLUMBER

An afternoon of napping and relaxation

Is like a short vacation

The house is quiet and peacefully calm

No more sweat upon your palm.

Your mind can float and visit the ocean floor

Where the beauty unlocks its door

Magnificent colors all around

Yet here there is so little sound

Gliding under water so spacious and clear

The wonder of it all soon to appear.

God's creation of all colors and life galore

He has them all in His store and more!

SMILE

Feel it, treasure it, enjoy your smile
Maybe it has been quite a long while.

There's nothing quite like it to make you feel grand
As you choose to take this stand

Be happy, enjoy this life of ours
The choice is yours, there will be showers

Of joy and pleasure as you start
Share your smile right from the heart.

All things will seem lighter
No time to be sad
Your world will be brighter
Your friends will be glad.

SNOW

A white coat of beauty

God spreads all around

As you gaze through the windows, not a sound

Thank God for our coffee and nice warm heat

A blanket to take the chill off our feet

All is frozen to prepare for the new

The same thing happens to me and you

Nature's way to teach us how to grow and be true

To ourselves

SPEAK

Speak with words of wisdom
Speak the bitter truth
Speak the words that cannot fail
Not the lies of teenage youth

Speak with love so gently
That all want to hear
Not with harsh, loud, angry words
Building only fear

Draw all friends and strangers close
Not so you alone can boast
But that we all may CHEER.

SPRING

Dust the dirt off everything!

As you can see, it is almost SPRING ...

Shine it well, make it glisten

Look outside and listen, really listen

The birds are singing, life is good

We are changing as we should

The bitter cold will leave us now

Once again

we can use the plow

Improve ourselves with each passing year

Knowing

SPRING IS ALMOST HERE!!!

STAND ON THE TRUTH

Stand on the truth

Get very close

Give yourself a "toast".

Always able to see the truth

Perhaps as you did in your early youth

Then habits came, your world bogged down

Turned your smiles into frowns

The lights are on, the truth is here

In your heart so very clear

Wake up! Think joy and liberation

A perfect day for celebration

Of the TRUTH!!

STAR

We're the star in our show

We will grow and grow and glow

Until we believe in who we are

Never listen from afar

Concentrating in the moment, we can be content

Sharing our lives with all, as we are heaven sent

Being just the best person we can

Knowing there is a finer plan

Taking one day at a time

As we travel this land divine

We are the Star of our show

This we surely know.

<u>STOP!</u>

The signs say "stop" yet you still proceed
Wait for My voice to fill your need!

Running along with blind will
Gives no time to instill

A better idea from His infinite mind
Yet He will always be kind

Let you travel along
In misery, no song

Until you tire and turn around
As you hear the wonderful sound

Of His voice, which is true
As it pours out within you.

SUBMISSION

There are times we need to submit to laws and people, too

No reason to be bitter or take time to throw a shoe

For most of our lives there is freedom and we can really choose

The steps we take to Destiny and we can never lose

Ups and downs will certainly be there

But we can live without a care

We must not submit to stopping here

Because our goal is so very near

Our destination becoming very clear

Look past those times of submission.

TEACH

How in the world can I teach you when I'm still teaching me?
This is truly my plea.

I can share the things I've learned the best that I know how
But in all truth, I learned from you, so may I turn and bow

That's why we are here, one in all, so together we may learn
Giving our knowledge to each other, showing our concern

We are working in a fantasy throughout this time of ours
Chasing all our dreams together, sending each other showers

Of truth, knowledge and so much more
Never, never keeping score
Always teaching forevermore.

THERE'S A SONG IN MY HEART

There's a song in my heart

We know it must start

As a wonderfully beautiful rhyme

It's declared from above

That we live in His Love

Sweet reflections are given in time

No more hate can we feel

For we know this is real

To be touched by His love so divine

Place your mind in His care

For He always is there

To make your life sublime.

TO BE ONE

To be one with God makes you completely whole

No negative ideas to be lived or told

Each day is a blessing to be grateful for

Each moment a gift like a shining bright star

There's no bickering, fighting, or waste of life

Delusions, killings, causing such strife

Joining our neighbors, united as ONE

No judging or scoffing under God's sun

He tells us all things. Are we listening?

To love your neighbor is the real thing.

Giving of yourself, all you can bring.

TREE

Watch it grow!

In the beginning really slow

Tender sprouts come out

With very few leaves about

Each passing year the stems will grow

Stronger and stronger to let us know

It will live life's course

Provide the special shade

It's call to life will soon be paid.

Our life story...

THE TRUTH

It seems to be so elusive

Do we really want to know?

Making life conclusive

Or simply be a show

They say the truth will set you free

Still most prefer to lie

Sometimes it's hard for us to see

Asking questions such as Why? Why?

We don't really want to know

So, we continue with our show.

WHAT DO WE WANT?

Happiness, love, we all want these things
With our judging thoughts, guess what they bring

Death, destruction, hate, separation
Thoughts without Love bring desperation

Love, joy, peace galore
They are the things we are looking for

Please, choose the thought that brings delight
Not one that shows only hate, no light

Relax enjoy this peaceful state
For this is truly God's gate.

Thinking thoughts of love for our fellow man
Is TRULY doing the very best you can

WITHIN

Let us take a look within to see what we can be

There is so much waiting there just for us to see

Programs from our childhood, people all around

Helped to make us who we are sometimes to astound

There are beliefs implanted though which need to be removed

Build our lives more honestly with positive words of truth

We will always grow and change making our life better

Our Destiny still remains itself right to the letter

Born with a very unique plan as we trod along

Now the time for us to sing God's very special song

As He teaches us to be very strong.

WONDERFULLY DIFFERENT

(My mentally impaired friend)

I was born one day

A little different, they say

Some look at me with their faces so sad

Say-What's wrong? You should be glad.

Just give me a coke and swing me real high

No reason to be gloomy with such a long sigh.

My life is my own and mostly you'll see

If you really look at me

I'm smiling a lot, probably more than you

(Though there are times you need to tie my shoe)

You should have my cares, no worries or strife

It's really quite fun, my life.

I appreciate the little things along the way

Which is something you may not always say

Do smile at me!! Let's laugh and play

I'm having an especially GREAT DAY.

BIRTHDAY

We've been told – a time to cry

The challenges of this life will come

Still the plan is that we learn to thrive

Not to yield and succumb

The strength we have is beyond our imagination

And yet if you listen to our conversation

The bad versus good

Is more understood

For we forget to remember our life

Even amid all strife

Is a celebration....

HAPPY BIRTHDAY !!

AFFECTION

Where did it go? How did we lose it?
We forgot one day just to choose it.

It is so warm and invigorating
So why in the world are we debating?

Sharing affection draws out all love
Centers our relationships with His precious love

Creates a whole feeling of strength and happiness
Affection brings with it true bliss

OUR HANDS

We can hold our arms out with hands open wide

Giving His love and affection to welcome others inside

Or we can choose to clench our fists, close the door to His love

Sharing anger, hate, separation, only shove and shove

Our hands are to embrace, hold each other close

With gentleness and care, tenderness we chose

IN HIS PRESENCE

His presence is in everything we see

The things of nature, you, and me

There is no face on Him to behold

He's that feeling of truth and comfort so bold

A warm, loving tingling as we start our new day

With our minds joined in His as we walk,

Come what may.

SOMETIMES

Sometimes it is hard to be honest

Sometimes it is hard to be glad

Sometimes it is difficult to be our best

Sometimes it is easy to be sad.

No matter the choices you make

Each day can be a true delight

Simply never, ever be a fake

Your honesty can bring true insight

Soon you will see

You were right !!

OUR HOME

A peacefully quiet place to read a book

A place to laugh, have fun, as we cook

A place to work and help one another

A place to make our bed, spread the cover

A place where cool, clear water flows

A place to wash between our toes

A place where harmony resides.

A place where you can come inside

We are thankful as you know

For here in God's love, we continue to grow.

FORGIVENESS

To forgive takes more strength than we sometimes have to give
Yet with hardened hearts unyielding, there is no joy to live

For each day we fail ourselves and others
Forgetting that we are all brothers

One in the universe complete together
How else can we, in this world, weather

The storms of life will always come to us
There's no reason to make such a fuss!

Forgiveness will come and cleanse our heart
Give us a chance for a brand new start

OPEN EYES

Open eyes carry with them all the love we have inside

As we look beyond the layers where bad habits often abide

Reaching past our judging spirits where His love resides

The surface of all things can be worn, scratched, and rough

Still if we look within, sometimes being a little tough

We'll find His presence – peaceful and pure

The outer self is just a bluff.

REALITY

If we should take a moment to hear our inner voice it would be an amazing feat. It is strong and powerful and filled with the joy of living. Still we sometimes choose to contemplate our own fate and not allow the inner power to show itself in our midst.

Take the hand of the Divine and trust it with all your being. Now your life will become united with His. Make no mistake about it. This is the way He intended each person of this universe to live.

He is not demanding, simply a still small voice offering us His way or the useless way of this world. Take a moment to LISTEN. Your mind will conform to His. Your health will return. Your life will improve. No effort on your part or stress. Just to move in whatever direction He leads.

It Is Finished...

Thank you for sharing your poem book with me. I wanted you to have this... I Love you, Susan

78